Jardinière

First published 2022 by The Hedgehog Poetry Press

Published in the UK by
The Hedgehog Poetry Press
5, Coppack House
Churchill Avenue
Clevedon
BS21 6QW

www.hedgehogpress.co.uk

ISBN: 978-1-913499-69-3

Jardinière

by

Kerry Darbishire

Contents

for Barbara

our times together

THE HOUSE OF LOST LAND

We might be anywhere but are in one place only –
Derek Mahon

Outside a door to birth and death asleep
in lath and lime, damp plaster walls
mapped in old ways of being, November

holds its breath, waits for a slow sweep
of the oak door to release a flock of songs,
conversations composted like leaves, lives

reduced to a trickle of water – the only
moving thing to wear away soured milk
from the flagstone floor, the to and fro of boots

distilled to air – locked-in air that knows only
the breath of horses, smell of fleece and cattle, land
now shrunk to a small parcel. We were warned

of a room low as a sailors' galley, beamed
against the easterly and rising mill race, the farm
gone missing but for a hearth of ash, petrified bees,

a child's cardboard ship cobwebbed
to the windowsill – painted white over
and over Georgian-green, the signature

of a hand pressed into the north wall
where we can't help but place our own

JANUARY

She wears the hours
wraps thin light
around her shoulders

holds the shortest days
like a new-born
dark eyes searching for light

skin smooth as an apple
small hands that grab
at promises.

Her voice willow-soft
weaves the longest nights
into low sun

and moon unveiled
to north-bound geese
slipping over

snow-bound fields
and hoarse hedges
beginning to sing

THE SETTLEMENT

Wear only the air today, warm
as a curlew's call, shy as sun in March.

Follow me past winter weed, song of a syke
frothing at the iron gate, sluicing clean
snowdrops torn, blackthorn bones
sharpened by the westerly.

Walk by briar – wands conjuring spring,
a currant bush, scent of a snapped branch, swans
idling on the tarn. Tread with care this field
slaped to bronze, gazing at a sky of gulls

mustering like iron filings, drawn to this fertile land.
Listen, pioneers are clearing trees, ploughing
earth, sowing seed. Take shelter under hazel rods
and straw where men and women

hone flint, patch daub, feed from the soil. Stand
with your back to the north and spitting hearth,
see beyond forgotten alder, evening shadows
shaping walls, a map of stars, here long before us.

A LIFE

Because it could have happened anywhere, why not here,
in the cold light of a northern winter – Elizabeth Burns

Why not here in a veil of wood smoke, clock
ticking, firm hand on his shoulder, the smell
of new-born lambs creased in his father's jacket
pegged to shadows. Here, sitting over revision-
papers scattered between dreams of the city
and steaming soup, his mother drifting about
the damp air, her voice soft, full of hope
for the farm

SPRING

THE SEEKERS

*A mason times his mallet to a lark's twitter listening
while the marble rests...* Basil Bunting

On a morning spring-soft and all that is Briggflatts
I tread in footsteps of the troubled
who three hundred years ago were welcomed
through the skin-scouring stone arch to the door –
iron-studded, heavy as a bull.

Campanula sneaks in behind promising blue,
aquilegia steeple-tall, pink for bees.
Swallows swoop to safety of the eaves
and in the lime-cleansed porch mapped by years
of dark day lanterns, I wonder at such faith.

Inside the hall, I choose the back to sit and peer
unnoticed through rows of Sunday caps and hats
and mourning black – that smart attire
hung neat on pegs of oak – trees felled and planed
and fed by trusting palms, hands that leaned

and prayed upon forgiveness on stormy days.
Believers who came by horse from Sedbergh,
Millthrop, Winder, Crook, to kneel on earth
before the creak of boards or lights switched on
to see folk through their happiness and grief.

Beyond the flax-high lane, I see Rebecca Langle's
buried here, the first to mark the yards of graves
where arnut blooms white as children's bonnets
dropped between those folk asleep
and mossed in chosen plots:

Allan Thirnbeck, William Hunter, Elizabeth Seddon,
Isaac Handlen reunite in hymns of blackbird, thrush
and wren, chorus of sycamore, copper beech where hope
faces south with each season's rise on Holme Fell, where
    Basil Bunting's moon held sway the trust

in *God's love available to all.* Lent lilies spent and eglantine
to flower, a splash of fallen sky spreads blue in bells
and scent of distant may along ploughed rows
of farriers, farmers, blacksmiths – Quakers
    who waited for belief.

CARRIED ON THE HELM WIND

How are we to know when seeds are planted in our heart?
To know if seedlings are perennials until years later lying

dormant they return to catch you off-guard one spring evening,
the scent of bluebells, narcissi in snatches

carried on the Helm wind and you're back tearing open
tiny packets full of wildflower seeds,

pouring the promise of yellow, blue and pink
into the palm of your hand,

learning the trick of mixing with sand to spread them further
imagining green shoots rising like tides

to the swell of moonshine hours
flooding your neat patch of freshly turned soil.

WOOD ANEMONES

Anemone Nemorosa

I could lie all night
in clean white sheets

starry canopy nodding
as I dream

of mice and voles
passing close as breath

from nests to moss
and back to the river's edge

foraging the dawn
gathering strength

LESSER CELANDINES

One celandine opens her throat
eight-petals to a sunbathed sky

then another and another butter yellow
butterfly yellow a glistening dawn

a lawn so full no foot no mouse or bee
can pass between their heart-shaped leaves

leaves some tear out   but here they stay
so I can swallow in the day

drop by drop them on my tongue
sing their tiny yellow song.

SEVENTH SPRING

I give thanks for my seventh spring
the girl in pink ribbons
who laughed at my accent
            on the school bus   and stole my smile.
                        Thanks for lonely walks home
                        river's glistening skin   reaching out
                                to take the weight of doubt
            wash it clean in splashes of sun through leaves.
Thanks for leaves   flowing red
whispering   *things can change*   as they fall.
For petrichor after heavy rain
            ferns wet as tongues
                                dripping kindness and green.
                        Thanks for trees   shelter
                the comfort of evenings poured into books
            my den of pages opening like wings
to other kingdoms.
I give thanks for those early winters
the height of wild geese
            slicing through blue silk
                                            to find softer light
                                                above snow
                                snow   falling in the night
                silencing deep cuts   taut scars
a girl left behind without knowing.
I give thanks for wounds
their grace   their strength
            to heal.

FROM THIS DEEP LAND

Yet with these April sunsets, that somehow recall
*my buried life...*T.S. Eliot

Let's rise like the highest notes of the river
and fly through descant of deeper air,
ride the north-eastern stars: Alioth, Megrez,
Dubhe, Merak, Phecda, Alkaid, Mizar.

> Let's be guided far from conversation,
> unopened letters on hard tiled floors
> and glide summer-high intakes, by edges
> bracken-green – folds beyond the snowline

sharp wild voices of fox and deer,
the cairn where we shelter each Solstice
unpack sandwiches and wine
to watch the sun rise. Let's rise like the sun,

> the ghost moon, the way wood smoke rises
> without fear of falling from this shining height.
> Let's not weed borders, clean cupboards, pour tea
> into china cups while the scent of white lilac drifts

the cobbled yard reminding us each April
to shed our winter manners. Let's fly
through the stars in soft frocks, light as wrens, rise,
sing like rivers.

BECK MOSS

Saunter the path   wool-soft
    haunch-wide
       ferns   thistle   watermint
pressed   aside
   by   heron   fox   deer
      footprints   mired fresh

to mud   like fossils bedded in rock
   Follow the rill
      down to a whisper
the lightest cloth
   thrown
      over the day

the way
     sedge warblers and damsels   dance
       wings-a-blur
through   scots pines
    lime-smirred larch
       bowing to the lapis blue

of devil's-bit scabious
    sleet grass seeds
      and butterflies
buried in thickets
    bog myrtle   reeds
      waist-deep   fidgeting

for release
     from the anchor
       of winter

HARESTONE

Beyond cowslips trembling in the Helm wind
  two hares preen shy coats.

Shadows play like children's hands
  against the mossy dry-stone wall –

the snow-line boundary east to west
  through Peter's intake to the stream,

where farm lads with their weathered hands
  hefted boulders, heartings in hawthorn air

and set the slab to bridge the squeeze
  of rabbit, stoat and hare.

IN PRAISE OF HEDGES

Good bones grown to last and burn long into autumn nights:
    ancestors   protectors   winter larders
        raided by axe, storm and hailing gnaw.

Do we take them for granted   not notice how
    by late spring these dishevelled umber skeletons
        become rulers and glorious?

Have we forgotten a father's track still warm in his before
        spelled belonging   hefted lads laying blackthorn hazel and haw to
keep lambs in and cool?

Have we mislaid the scent of rain   company of leaves
    shelter after school   the labouring on for weeks up the fields then back
to pleach and mend the gaps   the eager tap-echo-tap rhythm
    drumming the valley a call to prayer palls of incense signalling burning
brash   sweat of intakes
starlings turning February skies   jet
    then silver   with the promise
        of sun on young necks?

Can you recall the sound of bees   each bird-song   held
    in arms of blossom
        snowing the ground?

MAPPING WALNUTS

Today fat green buds are unfurling
from winter-grey branches of the walnut tree
and we're opening the last jar of pickled walnuts.

But it's not the slicing through months
of marinated fruit to expose the intricate image
of itself, the sweet and sour on our tongues, the sight
of our harvest laid on a blue plate next to cheese,
but the day we planted the gift of small fine roots
and tender boughs to the sound of the river.

The second year a branch ripped in the wind,
we almost didn't stop the bleed of sap, and watched life
drain and drain back into the earth,
saw how close death can come.

Three years later the first flowers set.
We spent weeks pacing, watching small green balloons
appear and grow. Some we harvested in July
to brine and pickle, some we left to ripen
hard on the branch to share through December.

Twenty-six years on this is not just a Broadview walnut tree
but my children small, learning the split of husks
in October, mature branches taking the strain of wily greys
plotting an early morning feast, trays of walnuts
drying in the sun, finding shells along paths to the fell.

NAOMI'S PASCHE EGG

I watch my daughter cut wet string
binding the purple-dyed linen to her egg
chosen from her favourite hen's cache
of new-laids. Still warm from inside the ark,
she cups and slowly carries it precious
as a fledgling just out of the nest.
On a morning-warm table of flower petals
and rising steam, she unpeels the tied cloth,
her small fingertips green and light as seedlings.
In held breath
she reveals a garden fit for Fabergé:
umber undergrowth of onion skin, fans
of primula wanda, primroses, lovage
and daffodils interwoven in a spring border
only she could plant.

MONKSHOOD

Wolf's-bane, Leopard's bane, Mousebane, Women's bane,
Devil's helmet, Queen of poison – Aconite

Early summer I wait for delphiniums' wild brothers
to appear outside my window, lime-green sprigs

to slip through soil like the necklace of wolf bane
Mina wore to protect her from vampires.

I listen for the murmur of tuber roots solid as coffins
to spread their deadly weapon between children's play

and spent daffodils. I watch them grow, poisonous javelins,
flowers blue as summer skies I arrange in vases.

I try to dig them out, make way for poppies,
wallflowers, larkspur, but they refuse to leave

telling me their nectar is needed for long-tongued bumblebees,
caterpillars, moths, my protection.

IN THE AIR

What if this should change?
The crab apple in blossom
leaning on a hawthorn like an old friend.
The brown and white cows cudding the lush meadow
beyond the wall. The rumble of John's tractor
checking ewes and lambs.
Tyres weaving morning's dew.
The hedge of May like brides in wedding gowns
beneath a lucky blue sky.
What if this should change?
These thistles pushing through turf
keen as fans at a football match. My dog,
nose to ground tracing every drop of last night's musk.
The resident owl who never seems to sleep
calling from the ghyll where the Plough always stops
between two sycamores and the smell of weather stays sharp.
The first swallows leaping air at finding last year's nests
in the barn. Orange tips giddying bluebells by the river
playing last night's rain. The cheeky pair of squirrels
darting up the trunk of the pine. The cocky pheasant
parading his apple orchard. What if this should change?
Bracken brushing green over the fell
where my children found bleached skulls
and the distant estuary gleams like a star, here,
where winter follows footprints through gorse,
where deer and fox graze unafraid.
What if I never hear their bark again?

SUMMER

ONE SUMMER

between tea laid on the table,
Heartbreak Hotel and my mother's frown,
I turned and walked
into the hottest evening of the year.

Air charged, world on fire –
the pavement, trees, even the river asking,
who is this man? voice deeper
than a midsummer sky,

eyes that could suffocate a classroom
of girls, hair so neat every lad
on our street thought they were *The King.*
And though I heard he was banned

from the waist down, I practised
his lip and hip moves on the lawn.
Radio Lux' carried him to my bedroom,
Love me Tender between the sheets. Elvis,

you ain't nothin' but a hound dog, you
broke a storm inside, raced fast as a rabbit
through my heart, ripping and digging
the deepest hole 'till it hurt.

WHEN I HEAR *LOVE ME DO*

I'm on the edge of the assembly hall
with Margaret, Nancy and Marion
expecting something more than a guitar lick
    at the school leavers' disco.

A reflection kicks back – PVC mini skirt,
purple tights, black polo sweater bragging
the Quant look – Sassooned hair
    that took me hours.

Vimto fizzes our tongues,
we're mods, we eat twiglets,
scan the floor for talent, the air is ozone –
    a storm is breaking

and the beat spins in my head
like a trapped bird whirling
an exotic perfume that could be mine
    I know who I am, I know.

Dreams of romance ring the room
like a thousand butterflies, I'm fifteen
I can dance – I'm flying
    without falling.

THE SALMON

What can I say about the salmon
garnished in green, gleaming
on a blue and white platter. All morning
my aunt intent on making the fish
look like a mermaid, sliding slices of cucumber
around like best silk.

Too late to slip back to sea
doomed to an heirloom charger
surrounded by florets of parsley
set in the centre of the table like an open coffin
outshining sausage rolls, egg sandwiches
and vol-au-vents.

My sixth birthday, getting in the way
of Aunt Mary's gas stove on legs, fish kettle balanced
at a simmer, bay leaves, peppercorns
and sticks of celery turning eerily in eddies of stock,
surfacing, sinking, circling the grey scaly skin,
her steamy chitter-chat hustling me out

to the garden, uncle Jack moving
white plastic chairs from the shady side
of the lawn to the other as clouds lowered
like a lid and the barbeque went out, my aunt still
arranging cucumber in party frills, guests hovering
not knowing whether to pray or dive in.

ABRACADABRA AISLE 4

What child wouldn't want this 6-string –
real Lyndon plywood top and sides, maple
fingerboard made-in-China guitar?

Appearing like a trick

between the electric hedge trimmer, Disney
frozen bubble tubs and paint stripper.
Smart enough to dissolve the tarnish of office work,

rent, a move up country, married
to pick-axing gardens, hacking plaster off
damp walls back to a layer of summer.

A good summer sitting for hours
on my grandmother's July-warm steps:
new-build semis, proud as polished halls,

netted windows, neat-striped lawns, pink geraniums,
Fox's Glacier mints stashed in gloves of Morris Minors
parked in matching drives belonging to names

like Doris, Mr Mitchell, Edie – neighbours too nice
to complain of me *Singing the Blues* over and over, G-C-D
hard-learned on my 4-string plastic guitar, ten-year-old
shyness vanishing into leafy air.

CROSSINGS

Car! my brother shouted
as we raced across the lawn to the gate
to watch it drone by. I knew the sound.
I knew the lorries rumbling nose-to-tail
loaded with stone giants dragged from the mountainside
and carted to the mill over the Brathay – tunes
that echoed, saws whining through wet slate,
water in spate white as a gander's back, cackle of jays,
jackdaws, cool breeze through apple leaves
and all summer the café bell ringing for scones and tea.

An Indian bell bought at a sale with a grandfather clock
ticking over exotic birds and rare flowers to chime
the hour, the school bus and bedtime.
It was the time of owls, Mr Benson's tractor
scaling and baling hay under gathering clouds,
September rain against the kitchen window, tap-tap
of Mr Fleming's white stick on the lane.

I to and fro between the bell dulled to my shelf
and bonfires charging November air, my mother
calling us in from an autumn garden, my captain father
turning fritters in a burnt pan, his slippers like boats
crossing calm lakes of lino.

THE LONG SUMMER

after Philip Levine

All summer I carried fear
fear of being late, fear of making a mistake.
All summer I slogged up the hill past my friend's farm,
watched her riding her pony as I cantered
the half-mile lane, stomach churning,
heart racing towards the hotel.
The grave hallway stilled by the smell
of tea and lavender, tall gaping mouths
of windows I learned to clean with vinegar-water
and newspaper. Eileen, starched white and waiting
to hand me instructions for the day, Mr Hawks
the owner, shuffling past not speaking,
not knowing how much death was in his eyes.
I imagined him sleeping in his three-piece tweed suit
hanging like terrible weather about his bent back.
I was allowed only once in the drapes-drawn
bedroom, his wife, a prisoner, lying in a weak veil.
I was fourteen, had only seen dead mice
and two run-over cats. All summer
I learned to lay tables, fold napkins into swans,
how fussy some guests were, what it was
to be a servant. My legs ached
climbing those stairs to spend an hour alone
in an attic room, distant light through a postcard window.
I saw a different view of the village, saw clouds
turn day into night, watched rain on roofs
and the church steeple shine like rivers. All July
wondering why was I hidden from summer.
Was it the blue dress in Taylor's window?
The day trip to Morecambe? Is this how life
was meant to be? Did my mother want me out
of the house, for what seemed an eternity?

DRIVING HOME

I could go back to the beginning, like the fox
sloping thin through privet hedges and side street bins
as if she's invisible, draining leftovers between
those restaurant goer's mizzled footsteps.

Windscreen wipers kick and clear my view
of closed-down shops, double yellows, the homeless
I can't help from the heat of my car, Bryan Ferry's
Slave to Love pulsing this vixen-eyed dashboard,
blood-lights from the car in front pumping fast as my heart.

I jam my brakes just as the fox clears a wall –
sleek fur burns bold as flames leaping
from a pine forest no-one can control, her tail
steering to circle the same place over and over

like me, always driving back to a place:
Christmas glowing from windows, an animal
creeping into our warm bed as we lay sleeping,
a storm howling at the door
not knowing how close it was.

LISTENING TO GORECKI ON HYDRA

her bench   the sun-bleached arms we fell into
apricot walls   the heat we craved
following a long northern winter

our feet rubbed sore by the donkey-slow hill
soothed by a succulent leaf she snapped off
the aloe vera   a cool stream over our burning skin

our first time here   terra cotta roofs shimmered
like ovens   we stared into the blue chiffon haze
sea and sky melting into each other

a sorrowful song soared away on gulls' wings
ocean-deep cellos rose above the miles we'd left behind
silencing our hearts

DISCOVERING FEDERICO GARCÍA LORCA

In the Andalusian mountains
under pure sky
     falling like lavender into the sea
I sit on this terrace near a pot of basil, notebook open
thinking of pesto and poetry.
         Across the valley olive groves
and lemon trees bracelet hillsides –
    steep and studded with hamlets
        threaded by chalk-marked roads
where last night four motorbikes
    revved up Saturday freedom –
           searchlights on the future.
I imagine Federico's mother Vicenta   waiting
at a table laid   dusk   severing
all dreams of her son
becoming a pianist like her.

        Scent of jasmine stirs the terrace,
      oranges hold green, almonds pop
   like tongues stiffened
by the drawn-out summer
and I'm under a robe of stars
stars that witnessed the poet's sudden end.

Land begins to sparkle gunfire   after   gunfire
down to the sea's mouth.
   I'm eating a salad of watermelon
manchego in olive oil
     tabasco
       and lemon.

I'M NOT IN LOVE

The names of the villages
belonging to that summer
escape me, but I remember
cramming the car with a tent,

sleeping bags, a dog, two children
the only cassette we could afford
and setting off for Wales.

Our first holiday, the song
that almost didn't happen,
rolled us along lanes, woods
by glimmering lakes, you smiling,

hand warm in mine mile after mile
past rivers smooth as the lyrics
and chords whispering hours to minutes

the sun tipping pine trees lipstick pink
until by starlight we could barely see
the road signs, unpronounceable
beginning and ending in 10cc.

BIRTHDAY

for Rebecca

I hear you're journeying friends
into the underworld, guiding them

through deep places to disentangle roots
blocking their way forward.

I always knew one day you'd leave
like Persephone stolen by Hades from her meadow.

I hear you moving among husks
below my feet, collecting seeds from flowers

you bought to our table after school.
You're mixing pigment, scent, dipping brushes

into cadmium, rose madder, manganese blue,
shifting bluebell bulbs, clover, bistort in the dark.

Today is your birthday,
the first time we cannot be together.

A RED ADMIRAL

The summer before you lay down
cobwebbed to my windowsill,
I watched you with the painted ladies,
clouded yellows, small blues, orange tips
giddying among poppies, monkshood
and honeysuckle, landing light as air
the same that carried you night
and day from Africa –

the distance I voyage, the high
and low notes – currents of hope and fear
for my children, their children, deep things
that surface, flit and bombard me
in a kaleidoscope of wings in flight
following the hues of my life.

AUTUMN

TO AUTUMN

Nothing has died
just absent for a while from fields
of midges and rain - intakes
silage-striped like summer dresses
       outgrown.

Despite the vacancies
in eaves, woodsheds and lime-light byres,
no swallows fetching, delivering
to hungry mouths in mud houses
       dry as hay,

nothing has died. This marketplace
of rosehips, rowan and elderberry still goes
about its business - selling to robins, wrens - winter
in their bones, staining stomachs, gate posts,
       our hands.

And even if in the hush of autumn chill
apples hang picture-still as glittered bells
in low orchard sun,
and leaves fall frail
       as feathers

through bramble-scented air
barely breathing in decaying lanes
of willowherb fraying dust
to earth, nothing has died
       just absent.

BLACKBERRIES

We picked enough blackberries
to jelly, crumble, jam, syrup
and stain the children's hands
for weeks. Last night
we walked back
up the brambled fell
to find fruit bloomed,
shrivelled, snatched
by a low October moon
swollen
      sinking
            pink.

SEPTEMBER 20TH 2019 ˜ GLOBAL CLIMATE STRIKE

In the boughed September-slow morning
a pair of skylarks giddy above the rusty fell – spin
and soar to specks of dust. A buzzard hovers,

swallows feed their last over thistle-cast fields,
butterflies paint gorse through rowan and blackberry air.
A squirrel skitters the snow-line wall towards

a thicket of hazels, stops, backtracks, stones
holding past and future. Dogs at my feet
don't want to run or say goodbye to the sun's gentle hands.

Rain is forecast but not in Botswana
where now horses, hippos and buffalo
are heaving their bones thin as hope

through parched plains, following dry lines
sinking to their necks in paths of mud to find
no water. Today wherever there is light in the world

streets are flooded with strikers, saviours
who don't want the earth to die.

IN THE SILENCE

Thickness   of dreams   raw-edged   unravel   and
spin   away   quick as the spider's threads above me   sharp   as a blackbird's
song   cutting   land   waiting for dawn   pale linen   to be
drawn over fields   and streams   by an invisible   hand

SILENCE

Sometimes we search for silence

in prayer, meditation, but always
a kestrel will be calling, a blackbird
hungry amongst haw berries, a robin
will follow you singing like a stream.

Imagine an Autumn garden

not drawing attention to itself:
phlox nodding with bees,
a warm breeze through the willow,
the late hum of insects in the cotoneaster.

Sound comes looking

from a grave, from a page when you least expect. Something
is always telling us something. Somewhere
a tide is shifting pebbles on a shore, a clock
striking the hour, a fox barking on a fellside.

Even snow carries sound through the greyest sky.

In this soft September afternoon
I hear a leaf hitting the ground,
lovage seeds spilling over a path.

IN THE CORNER OF A CAFÉ

he unrolls a river from around his neck
scent of fells   an early summer   high song
of curlew   fox and flights of geese.

She unzips a path through her skin
tree roots whispering to each other   stones
worn smooth   embedded in sixty falls

of autumn leaves   a jigsaw scattered to the ground
she pieces together   watching his nightfall eyes
fathoming her sea-greens – shades of the day

they met. Coffee arrives. Rain drips from umbrellas.
They pour out moonlight, sonatas, coastlines. I lip-read
pretending not to. He peels bracken from his back   she

slips her jacket over the chair   her hair a waterfall
where they swam in evenings of cuckoo
and willow rippling the surface. Coffee steams   air fills

with wild geese tearing   mending   navigating
storms   the mountainous way they touch   let go
over moorlands of heather on fire.

THE SNOW GOOSE

after Paul Gallico

Stained with redcurrants picked to make jelly, her hands
slip over the pages, turning them like goose wings
across *marshlands and saltings... the crooked meandering arms
of many little rivers whose mouths lap at the edge
of the ocean.* My mother in her dress, borders
of flowers, perfume caught in the cotton-weave
of every evening. My sister and I tucked up, waiting
for the *greys and blues and soft greens* in the loneliest sky,
waiting to breathe the salt breeze through our pillows.

Outside the garden has fallen invisibly dark,
the colour of a stormy sea. Her voice is rain
drenching a parched field. Her slim fingers follow each line
like a painter sizing up a blank canvas
or a pianist along keys. *In his retreat,* she reads,
he had his birds, his painting, and his boat. We know
what's coming but pretend to forget. She must say it.
Her body edges towards *the tidal creek and estuaries
and out to sea.*

She sweeps her hair off her face, takes a breath
I hear birds crying to come home. We wait
for *the rushing noise of their passage...*the many hundreds
that stayed with the man on the shore.
He tells us through the cold weather, they *answer
the call of the north in the spring, but in the fall
they would come back, barking and whooping and honking
in the autumn sky...* just before the child with deep
violet eyes, carries *in her arms a large white bird.*

My sister buries her head under the eiderdown...
and it was quite still, my mother continues,
There were stains of blood on its whiteness and on her kirtle
where she had held it to her. Show me a picture, I ask.
She lowers the page of geese flying over a lighthouse,
watches my face for approval. Her name hand-written
inside, distance clinging to the last words I still hear
in my sleep... *Only the frightless gulls wheeled*
and soared and mewed their plaint over the place
where it had been.

.

WEBS

They keep coming back
to trap me into reading diaries
and notebooks woven by my mother.

Lists she wrote, plans made, pages
of to-do's in delicate handwriting –
s's and g's neatly spun.

Small reminders: tidy the kitchen,
walk the dog, feed the cats, buy tea,
Ink-marks for Wednesday 3pm, Friday 10am,

pick blossoms in the garden,
books to the library, lists – poems jotted,
loved, forgotten.

Words she threaded together but couldn't recall.
I should have wiped them out, her voice
on the phone twenty times a day before

falling prey to feeling small, tangled,
catching dust.

THE WINDOW

A small bird perches on the kitchen chair,
timid, full of hope, looking back
at the way it flew in - the window someone closed.

I remember my mother alone, holding on,
watching her fingers flick like chaffinch wings,
dreaming of her garden.

I wander past the dog sprawled on the red sofa,
photos of my children, shelves of poetry
and carry on upstairs, return to the highest room,

just as I left it - Rembrandt-dark, scent of lavender,
wooden floor silent, a candle, ceramic horse for company,
my notebook abandoned open at the page

of good intentions. The day I would write
until sunlight bursting through the attic window
was all that mattered.

.

THE WINDERMERE CHILDREN

on hearing Helen Mark's The Lake District Holocaust Project   *- BBC4*

In 1945 three hundred children had nothing
to go back to. *Coming here was like going from hell
to heaven, a journey to the moon,* said Samuel Laskier –

the Polish Jew who spent seven months in Auschwitz
before taking the worst journey imaginable
to Theresienstadt concentration camp. *I was lucky,*

that's me, the little one in the middle, he points
to the scuffed black and white photo of refugees,
arms around each other, flesh on their bones,

sun on smiling faces, Wansfell rising like a mother swan.
*We'd lost our parents, childhood and education.
It was a hot summer, we had no clothes. For ages*

I walked the street nervous, looking behind me.
Water laps the shore of Lake Windermere. Yachts
and rowing boats weave the surface of a lost story.

I can't measure my childhood from his, can't fathom
how I walked freely without fear, can't see
for the weight of rain.

Seven decades on buttons are still arriving,
they've nearly reached their target of six million –
the number of Jews killed in the Holocaust.

Most of his comrades gone, at the reunion he tells
of the Army trucks waiting at Carlisle airport to transport children
aged three to sixteen, to Calgarth – a *place of beauty, clean sheets
and even a little bar of chocolate.*

Theresienstadt – a concentration camp in the Czech Republic

IN HONOUR OF EMILY WILDING DAVISON

The Suffragette - 13ᵗʰ June, 1913

To believe with a passion in women's liberty
is to rise early, wash, wear a best dress and jacket,
take time with your hair, roll and pin it under a good hat,

lace boots, make sure your handbag contains
a return ticket to London, two flags, a race card, a ticket
to a suffragette dance later in the day, not forgetting

a diary with appointments for the following week.
To believe in equality for women everywhere
is to be prepared to die but not mean to but be armed

with hunger strikes, imprisonment, know
what it's like to be force fed – a tube rammed
down your throat then hosed in your cell until

you're locked in six inches of freezing water.
To pay the ultimate price of freedom
is to lay down your life, be glorious, stand

unnoticed in the crowds on the final corner
of the Derby race track, wait for the ground to drum,
walk out, clip a WSPU flag to a horse, even if afterwards

they say,
the King's horse was pure happenstance.

FALLING SILENT

Jaqueline du Pré 1945-1987

From the heart of the old wood
   a hundred birds flew
      singing of streams   skies   dawn –
passion taking flight
   as if nothing else was so alive
      as if they were drunk on something wonderful
like love was all here.

And my father   eyes closed   head tilted
   to the evening radio
      my mother stopping everything
to steal a moment of the Delius 'Cello Concerto
telling me
      this sound is blood   *making everything possible.*

And I too young to know why
   one beautiful October day my mother cried
      and cried for *the golden girl*
in her bluebell-blue silk dress playing as if she'd invented music
   running with nature   wild   trusting   imagining
      everyone was like her   that this
         could go on forever.

WATCHING HER DROWN

She fumbles her cardigan buttons smooth,
gazes out at a path veiled in mist, asks if I'm ready for school
then points to trees and flowers she cannot
     bring to the surface.

A mother who could dig up a hundred stories,
taught me yes and no, even distractions I use now
to mend the fraying cord between us: weather,
     shopping, jokes in hope of a rescue.

I visit her every Friday. We drink weak coffee
in an overheated room, arrange mementos
along a varnished shelf like stolen valuables.
     When am I going home?

We dust china dogs and photos that refuse her names
of babies, birthdays, fells and tarns – cold as the day
I broke my promise to save her from drowning
     in a murky high-winged chair,

the day the consultant asked,
Who is the Prime Minister?
What year were you born?
What day is it?

MEMENTOS

From a room flickering coal light
before I was born where they came
and went talking of new plays and reviews
over sweet sherry poured sparingly, where love
and fear ricochet worn carpets, beige-papered walls,
reminders are gathering on my windowsill:

five pheasant feathers from Richmond Park,
a lead Scottie dog in no need of walks,
her white coat thinned to grey by packing case
after packing case, sadness carted in her eyes;
one newspaper cutting, again, no success notices
for *Housemaster* at the Coliseum, just thumbed print

holding back the sirens yet to come
and final curtain calls of all-but-one West End theatre.
And tucked in the corner, the wooden monkey
my father turned in the palm of his hand, perhaps
to draw the luck he needed. The monkey
he told me to keep, always, as if in turn

it would give me answers I still search for
years later, along November lanes –
in drifts of wood smoke, bird call,
a full moon beyond my window.

MY MOTHER'S HOUSE

The wooden rooms echoed
every bare thing: neat squares of dirt –
absence of mountains and moonlit lakes silver-framed,
the weight of a bees-waxed sideboard embedded
in the saleroom carpet I begged her to buy,
that damp smell – dogs she no longer recognised,
bedrooms hanging on to mumps, measles – illness
mended with teaspoons of malt and orange juice,
cobwebbed views to the river in all its moods,
the cellar pump coughing-up water from the well,
the felt roof leaking rain on to the piano – lid open – mum
playing us through the worst winters
until her fingers could no longer span
and the octaves fell silent. Years
distilled into a last hour I held
like best glass, touching every brailled wall,
my mother's fury close as breath, her sadness
slipped to numb hands, a smile
on the agent's face, measuring, calculating
a priceless thing.

THE HOUSE THAT GREW IN ME

The day I left
rain drizzled the felt roof
each window cobwebbed me out
orphaned to winter
beyond the garden gate,
guilt and sorrow
packed in the word
sold.

The day
I handed over
the heart-beat of wooden floors
over-painted walls
birdsong latched in the apple tree
scent of azaleas
tricks of the river
my mother's bruised skies
my father's bed of leaves
the key to
summer.

AT THE END OF THE DAY

The smell of vanilla and honey now gone,
her hands, her skin worn to thinnest cloth
embroidered blue, like the one she threw

like a fluttering sky across the evening table,
laughing clear as a vim-scrubbed sink
telling us about her day:

the delivery of pineapple ice-cream, cones
and wafers, sweets for the shop counter
we were allowed to stack, her batch of scones

and cakes all sold to passers-by. And late
after the last walkers had drained their cups
and left her garden of birdsong and river turning gold,

we had her back, back to ourselves.
I was eleven, my brother growing stupid
for girls, my sister already engaged –

those warm evenings before we were swept away
my mother breathing the sweet scent
of stories and rhymes

to carry me to the stars line by line
only to wake to afternoons turning pages
in the stillness of her room.

THE MOMENT

before the New Year
and snowdrops pierce the soil
　　before azaleas fully open and begin their slow death
and blossom falls
before birds fledge from safety
　　and swallows begin to break
the surface of my heart
before I sink into a clear river on the hottest day
　　before opening my exam results
leaving school
before butterflies begin their first flight
　　before you look back at me
your hand touches my shoulder
warmth reaches my neck
　　before we sneak back into the house late
like missing animals
curl into bed
　　and wake to the sound of a door closing
before I turn ten　　　sixteen　　　thirty
before the pregnancy test
　　before my waters break
and nothing will ever be the same

　　　　　　　　　　　　　　the moment

before we taxi the runway
　　for our first holiday
and I hold my children instead of you
before I notice the hours chiming
　　and they too have flown
before that second glass of wine
the smell of gin on your breath
　　and doubt sets in like the longest winter

before words fall like wounds
and are buried alive
   before my mother dies
and I know what death looks like
how grief behaves
   before I know what loss is

JARDINIÈRE

When I lift the lid I let go the ghosts
of kings and queens tombed in their paper-dry
beds – buds and petals still clothed in the palest dawn,
bonfire-grey, evening-sky-pink, thunder-cloud-yellow,
honesty's sheen like rainstorms that often sent us back
inside with the smell of drenched earth in our hair.
When I lift the lid, I could turn a field into a garden,
work all day, become Vita Sackville-West or
Gertrude Jekyll using her painterly approach to colour.
Season after planted season I grew, cut and gathered
aquiligea, rosa rugosa, alchemilla, poppies, larkspur,
honoured their brief blooms in vases until
they threw themselves down like confetti.
When I lift the lid, forty summers rise and wake
from slumber: lapsang souchong and cake, birdsong,
afternoons fading in deck chairs, slow-scented evenings
folded in the wings of moths, my daughter's tenth birthday,
the spring she broke her arm, the autumn she left home
and my mother fell ill. It is a thing to leave your soil.
When I go I'll take my garden with me.

HEAVEN

In a garden far from the Tian Shan Mountains,
cultivation of the Malus,
its journey along the Silk Road
to hybridisation, to a northern hillside
where we dug and found solace,

we planted Bramleys – keepers
no more than babies in neat rows clinging
to a sloping orchard, skinny limbs
dipping only with the weight of robins
landing for a christening in the wide uncluttered sky.

This morning among the fallen leaves,
I need no more than branches breaking,
low sun gathering old traces, air swollen
with September-full apples
longing to be pressed, jellied
and sliced for pies.

THE GARDEN

after Galway Kinnell

The girl picking up boulders in the field knows each curlew   kestrel
hare
their dark tracks through morning dew   knows their cries of hunger
mating and nest. The girl picking up boulders to build a wall   dreaming
of peonies and poppies   her first garden   stone   alive in her hands
glistening like new-borns   ancient as storms finding home in the earth.

Footings   boulders angled just right   heartings   throughs   and cams to
shed rain.
She's laying in sedum   ferns and moss – a barrier against flood   against
the high-pitched northerly driving-in words of snow. Her mother looks on
from the confines of her chair saying   *how tired you must be*   her
feathered voice carried on pastured air   and gone.

Into each   parched   summer   each harsh winter   the girl sinks
into the wall
mapped yellow with lichen   into mossy hollows   home to mice and wrens.
Stone   by   stone   she falls   weightless   bones calloused   gapped like
autumn hedgerows   letting in the cold   letting ragwort and meadowsweet
take over.

SAYING GOODBYE

for Barbara

Did the sky really look like that today
luminous as the inside of a shell?
Did I hear wind in the arms of the black-laced
sycamore, heading for a pale horizon?
I haven't moved from my room for remembering
your everything-is-possible laughter; the day
we scrambled through mist towards the copper mines
as if navigating a path to our future, the night
we were scared and slept on your floor to escape
the ghosts wandering our house, and shared our last
cigarette in the shadow of Low Arnside
and talked of when we are old like it was Jupiter or Mars.

Through these weakening autumn days
I imagine you drifting off for hours to Chopin, Debussy
notes rising from the sitting-room below,
your loved-one wrapping you in sounds of garden borders
and birdsong. Your old plaster walls steeped
in music, years of practise yet now he says
his hands are too slow for Liszt.
Am I being selfish to love you so much?
To ask, did you smell the last rose, wood-smoke
drifting up the valley? Could you hear the storm,
the river's brashness cascading past your garden?

Is it only three weeks since we bought cake, sat by the river,
colour in your cheeks as we talked about a swim
and fresh-water muscles? The sun was so bright
we even wore hats. This evening I watch rain
catch light on my window like a million stars.

WINTER

GUIDE TO WINTER

Let air drugged with frost
fall to the ground.
Listen to the slur

of summer words
at the feet of sycamores
curled in rime instead of green.

Let the moon be your lantern
to show you hills beyond your own
and the fox barking on the fell

remind you of the needs of others
searching for warmth
in the longest night.

Let a robin's song
be baubles on branches
the bells you hear

through veils of snow.
Leave gates and walls rink-smooth
islands of moss stranded

in winter's ocean. They will survive.
And through the rigours of each day
walk through the space

someone left behind.

SYCAMORE LEAF

Face down you lie
  dried to gravel edges of the lake
    shouldering rust

sunlight, night rain, birdsong,
  woodsmoke – drift of a year.

I think of us returning
  winter after winter, wanting back
    the easiness of green, summer

arms stretched to the sky
  your veined hands

running swift as rivers over me,
  your gift of flowers
    trembling under stars,

low strum of wind through those
  long sweet hours.

THE SMALL THINGS

To not see beyond but know it is there
is the maze I vanish through in the absence of freedom.

The narrow corridors I run my fingers over
as if guidance is hiding in leafy shadows,

these days disguised as a long winter, streets
and lanes struggling to find faith.

A squirrel has remembered seed on the bird table
and scampers towards it. A robin stakes its territory

in a flurry of feathers catching light
fast as Wren breath on boughs of the azalea

and buttercups smiling are determined
to see November through.

A flock of geese have found their way
across the Solway, their chatter falls

and sinks like oil into my skin, the balm
of this kingfisher-wing sky, hidden stars

sugared violets melting into the sea.
I've come a long way to breathe the same air

as birds, squirrels and flowers, to know
they're still there.

DARKNESS

With a cache of mist
and a nip under your arm,
you slink into the yard
hungry as a wolf.

You swallow our stack
of slates, wood and wire
to mend gaps, the last
warm breath of the day.

You dismiss the swish of owls'
wings like chimney rags swiping
wood smoke through sycamore
and stone.

Inside the lime-washed porch
you run your gloved hands
over bellied walls to an alcove,
powerless to stop a candle burning.

DECEMBER MORNING

During the second movement by Nigel Hess
on radio 4, I stop stirring brandy into cinnamon,
candied peel, cherries and raisins – a night sky
spiced with all the Christmases I remember:

sitting in my mother's tree-lit room,
her fingers like doves flying the keys
of her burr walnut baby grand.
Outside the mid-winter orchestra:

sleet on the felt roof, opus of swollen river
surging rocks, the bridge, gathering
to flood every runnel and dyke in the valley,
my mother smiling, eyes closed.

Mornings I can't alter – mincemeat cooling,
the presenter announcing, *even a florist
in Suffolk stopped to listen
in the middle of her arrangement.*

VEGETABLES AS THE MAIN EVENT

... could change the eater's whole view of vegetables –
David Canter

Happy Christmas Kathleen 1968 –
with love, written inside the scuffed pink
and brown cooking clips book.

Slim new pages grown fat
with soup, croustades, bakes
and casseroles shown in Woman's Own.

Ingredients scribbled on scraps of paper,
Mediterranean cuisine pocketed
to upgrade Granny's beef

and boiled cabbage. Stylish Cranks
Café recipes fussed over, folded,
swapped at village coffee mornings,

the school gate where bold mums
said *yes* to candlelit dinners to show off
spinach roulade, carrot layer, borscht –

daring combinations – new warmth
on our northern tongues: garlic croutons,
champignons à la Grecque, pasta primavera

torn from places she'd never been –
my mother's yen for *transpontine delights*,
her French onion soup I can taste now.

SKY-LINE

engraved like a swan flying across a grey dawn
     into mornings when I heard the wire whisk
          stirring eggs and milk into flour, my mother

standing over a bowl, her rosy pinny
     caked in a week's baking, her hands like a river
          whispering, *not long now.*

I keep it tied to a kitchen beam, watch it cast shadows
     as the sun creeps round. It's lost its shine
          but not the smell of fritters, smoke spiralling air.

Skyline: trade name for a whisk circa. 1950's

THE BAG

Hand-stitched blue half moon handles   still
taking the weight of half known things hidden

in a dark interior   how in fifty years
I never noticed your colours

falling softly into focus   orange   white
and green   embroidered flowers

flowers I've never seen in my garden   and the cart
pulled by a donkey through a night of stars

apartheid   scent of South Africa
hanging on to the chest of drawers

the woollen fringe that stained my uncluttered mouth
red   as autumn leaves   wet   as mist on the river

the day swallows left like skeins of wool   threading the sky
and my grandmother arrived by sea   with a gift

exchanging dry torn earth   for fields of frozen grass –
one more northern winter

TIME CAPSULE

The row of six houses remind me of a train –
a train going nowhere yet everywhere.

Well-oiled, contained, regular to the roar of the river,
pine tops, horses, carts, sowing, harvest, sun, snow –

seasons knowing when to appear
and when to leave, how much to give and take.

Like the passengers behind their netted windows,
I knew them all, their love and sorrow

going about the year collecting storm brash,
setting hearths, eating rhubarb and apples from gardens,

cooking suppers of trout, breakfasts bartered oats
for eggs from blind Charlie – the man with hens

who tapped his way home at precisely five o'clock
every day. And Mrs Clayton next door but two

with a gammy hip who took in mending on Fridays
and washing on Mondays, was happy

as swallows in spring. Folk who believed in nature
without broad-band, sleepless nights pondering

black holes or icecaps melting, forests and fells tinder-dry
or amber storms with names that steal fields and lanes.

One day I'll go back and dig up a brain, a pulse,
the heart of a village.

LETTERS FROM HOME

It's not your news
the willow-curve of your words
I wait for   but the space
between the lines

    clear taste

of the ghyll
her mouth-grey dawns   squall
of blackbirds   thrush and wren   echoing
the leaf-scorched beck

    her rain-on-rain September song

thrum of hooves
to shearing   dipping   cries of separation
banks of primrose   violets   lizards
storing summer warmth

    the pause

between dappled shade and tiny
dusty throats swallowing the moon
in love with her own gaze   her promise
to return on dead fern days

    that northern light

falling between the lines

    like winter from the sky

WINTER

after *Wolf Moon* – Mary Oliver

Now the months of beauty and the beast,
hungry robins and wrens
from their woven beds
like specks of ash at the bird table.

Now the months of opening
and closing curtains faster than slate rivers
whispering under icy skins, a wolf moon,
lazy suns bowled over dead lawns.

Now the months of choirs
in the chimney, cloaked at the door
luring us out to owls
haunting the grave hours before dawn.

Now the months of tangled roots,
hunkered rabbits and mice, snow-bound lungs,
bare-boned hedges moaning, snowdrops
lost to blindness beneath our feet.

Now the months of fields and lakes paralysed,
wild scent of pine, a sated hearth at its best
glowing peat, ash-yellow coal-blue begging us
to join their dance.

Now the months to dream of spells
and candles, steamy kitchens, marmalade,
a larder of books, dark days
waiting to be devoured.

SONG OF THE FELL

When you say fellside
a woodpecker drums spring
into the ghyll, curlews turn their tune
inland on salt clouds scudding west
to east fast as a fox crossing high slopes
where runnels of earth slip from lairs
    and whins begin to yellow the air.

When you say fellside
an evening in summer swims out
of my children's eyes as they race
to the beck where lizards soak up warmth
from boulders, foxgloves guard sheep trods
firm as stone, where reeds lean in like old friends
    and distance spreads a blue cloth.

When you say fellside
owls haunt low light, the first frost
snaps at hedges of hazel and thorn, snow
steals boundaries without a second thought
from high intakes at rest, hollow nests, berries
shrivel and all evidence of life before
    is squirrelled under white.

When you say fellside
celandines must be opening, a half-moon floating
in a lake-blue sky lifting sun, swallows
and flights of geese over Whinfell
our bright steps climbing a new path to find
water-mint, frog spawn, primroses
    waiting for rain.

RETURNING

...I was about to enter a place that existed only in the overlapping of air and water, light and time -Tan Twan Eng

I felt nothing had changed
evening air holding the scent of pine
sycamore and ash taking the weight of rain
river's wing-beat caught against rocks
                                    a blackbird
singing from the tallest damson
crooked against the sky soft as a flock of geese
azaleas loosening their pink frocks and I
had never gone far

FUTURE

Not the name of a rock band or someone I know
but more of a creature that lives forever. Rare.
Out of reach. Remote, yet the sound of it
rolling in my throat tonight as I breathe through
        an alteration of vowels, the word ... *future...*

begins to feel like a boulder. And in this restless night
I remember *Que sera sera* –
Doris Day's springtime voice inhabiting every cell
of my small body, full of hope, swaying like an unborn,
        cradled safe, ignorant of *whatever will be will be* –

the agility, the lightness of it on my tongue,
my mother giving nothing away, me too young to fathom
the hereafter, time-to-come, from here onwards
into days of reading tarot cards, the I Ching, stars
        in opposition to Nostradamus.

I'm almost afraid to open my lips, let slip
the weight of today and tomorrow
        knife-edged, precious.

ACKNOWLEDGEMENTS

I'd like to thank Mark Davidson of Hedgehog Poetry for publishing my third poetry collection *Jardinière*, which I'm thrilled was joint winner in the *Full Fat Collection* Competition 2021. Thanks to writing challenges during this year of Covid19, keeping me sane, planting new seeds of poetry and meeting new poets: Angela Carr's *Thirty Day challenge,* Cahal Dallet's *Between the Lines*, Anne Marie-Fyffe's *Solitary Spaces,* Angela Locke's *Super Group*, Anna Saunder's *Cheltenham poetry festival workshops.* Thanks also The Poetry School feedback surgeries, and The Poetry Business *Apart Together* zoom workshops which have been a vital source during this Pandemic. My thanks and appreciation to Niall Campbell for his valuable feedback. To Judy Brown for her encouragement and sound advice. To friends at The Brewery Poets, Dove Cottage Poets and Write on the Farm, for guidance and support. My thanks also to Carole Bromley, Joy Howard and Niall Campbell for their endorsements. Also my thanks to Jen Hartley, Caroline Taylor and George Needham of The Cumbria Opera Group for performing *Falling Silent* in their 2021 Lakeland Cycle tour. My thanks to Alan Rice and family for his kind permission to use a quote by Elizabeth Burns from *Lightkeepers*, Wayleave Press. And last but not least, my husband Steve for encouraging me every step of the way and for the painting on the front cover. I'm truly grateful to the following during this challenging year for publishing some of the poems within: *Hedgehog Press, Dawntreader – Indigo Dreams, Grey Hen Press, Words for the Wild, Icefloe, Places of Poetry, The Alchemy Spoon – Clayhanger Press, 2Meter Review, Finished Creatures, The NNicholson Society, Comet, Birmingham Journal – Pallina Press, Dreich chapbooks, Arrival At Elsewhere – Carl Griffin Against the Grain Press. Folklore Publishing, Ware Poets, Nine Pens Press, Atrium.* Several poems were placed first/second/third or short-listed in competitions: *Settle, Grey Hen, Wells, Canterbury, Poem and A Pint, Hedgehog Poetry – 'Songs' anthology, NN Society, Folklore Publishing, and Ware Poets.*

PRIZES:

The Window: 2nd prize in the Folklore Poetry Prize competition, 2020

The Settlement: shortlisted in the Grey Hen poetry competition, 2020

The Moment: highly commended in the Poem & A Pint competition, 2018

The Small Things: Shortlisted in the Brian Dempsey Memorial Prize, 2022

ALSO BY KERRY DARBISHIRE

A Lift of Wings – Indigo Dreams 2014
Kay's Ark – Handstand Press 2016
Distance Sweet on my Tongue – Indigo Dreams 2018
Glory Days – Grey Hen Press 2021
(a collaboration with Kelly Davis)
A Window of Passing Light – Dempsey & Windle 2021